YUM, YUM, YUM

YUM, YUM, YUM

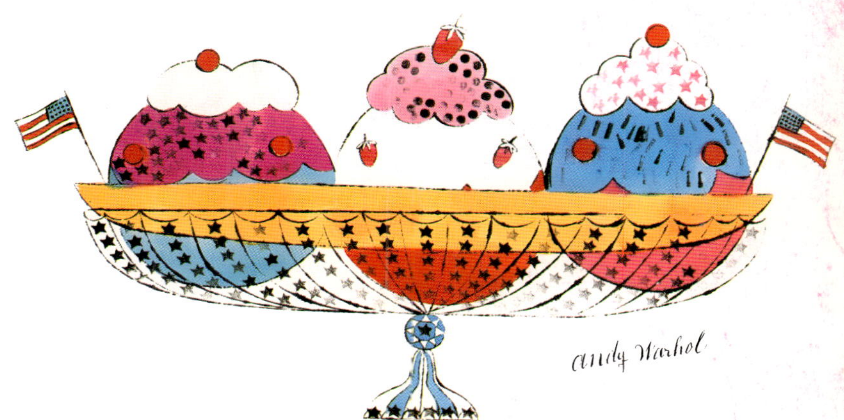

ANDY WARHOL

A BULFINCH PRESS BOOK

LITTLE, BROWN AND COMPANY BOSTON NEW YORK TORONTO LONDON

FIRST EDITION
Quotations from Andy Warhol compiled by R. Seth Bright
Designed by John Kane

Library of Congress Cataloging-in-Publication Data

Warhol, Andy, 1928–1987.
    Yum, yum, yum / Andy Warhol. — 1st ed.
        p. cm.
    "A Bulfinch Press Book."
    Includes bibliographical references.
    ISBN 0-8212-2133-7 (hc)
    1. Warhol, Andy, 1928–1987—Themes, motives. 2. Warhol, Andy,
1928–1987—Contributions in food. 3. Food in art. I. Title.
TX631.W25 1996
741.973—dc20   95-42871

Bulfinch Press is an imprint and trademark of
Little, Brown and Company (Inc.)
Published simultaneously in Canada by
Little, Brown & Company (Canada) Limited

PRINTED IN SINGAPORE

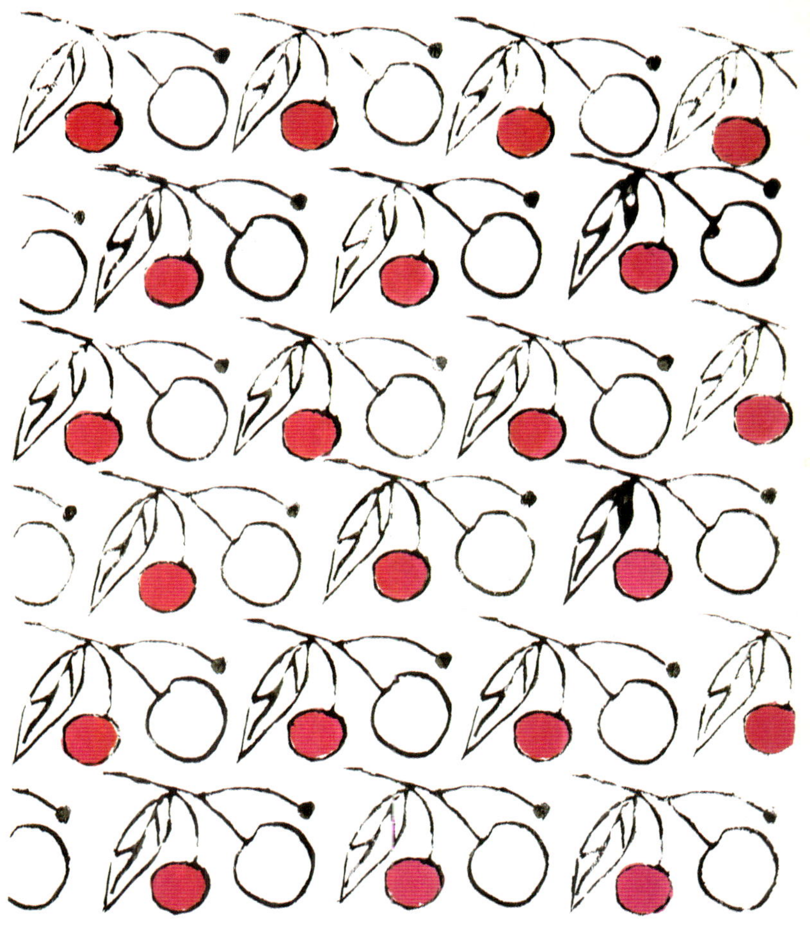

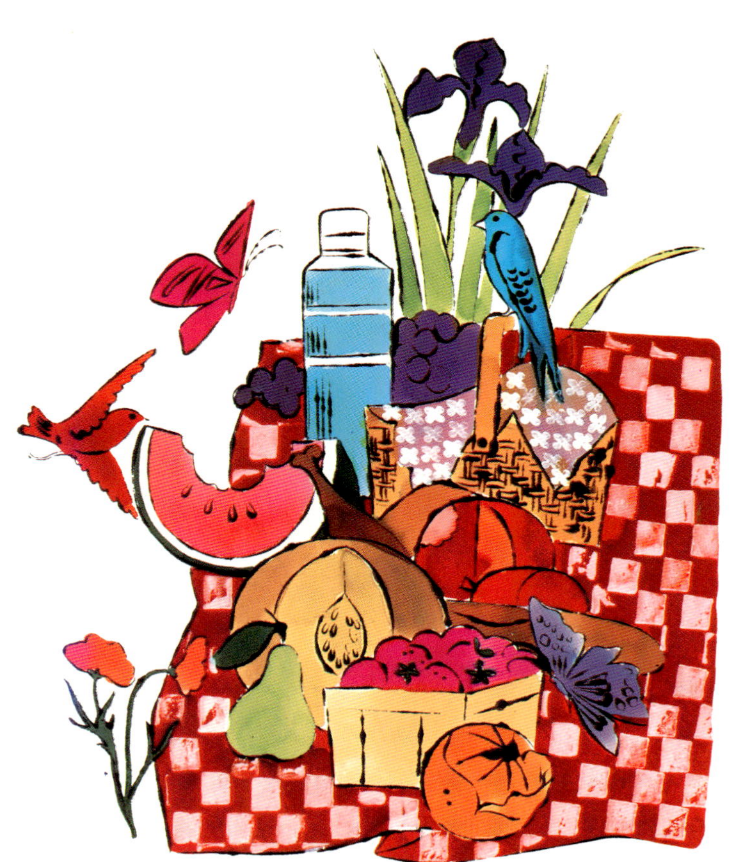

No matter
what changes
or how fast,
the one thing
we all always need is

real good
food

so we can know what the changes are

and how fast they're coming.

Food

is my great

extravagance.

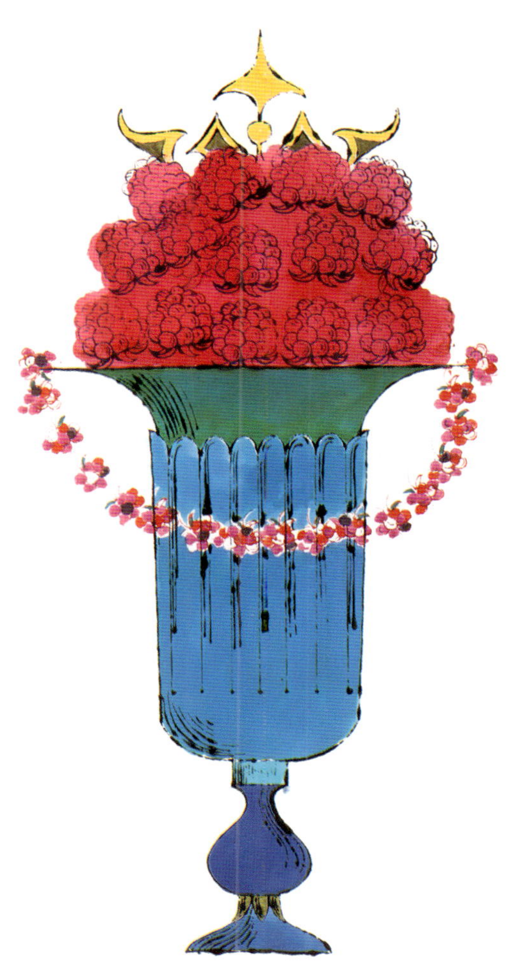

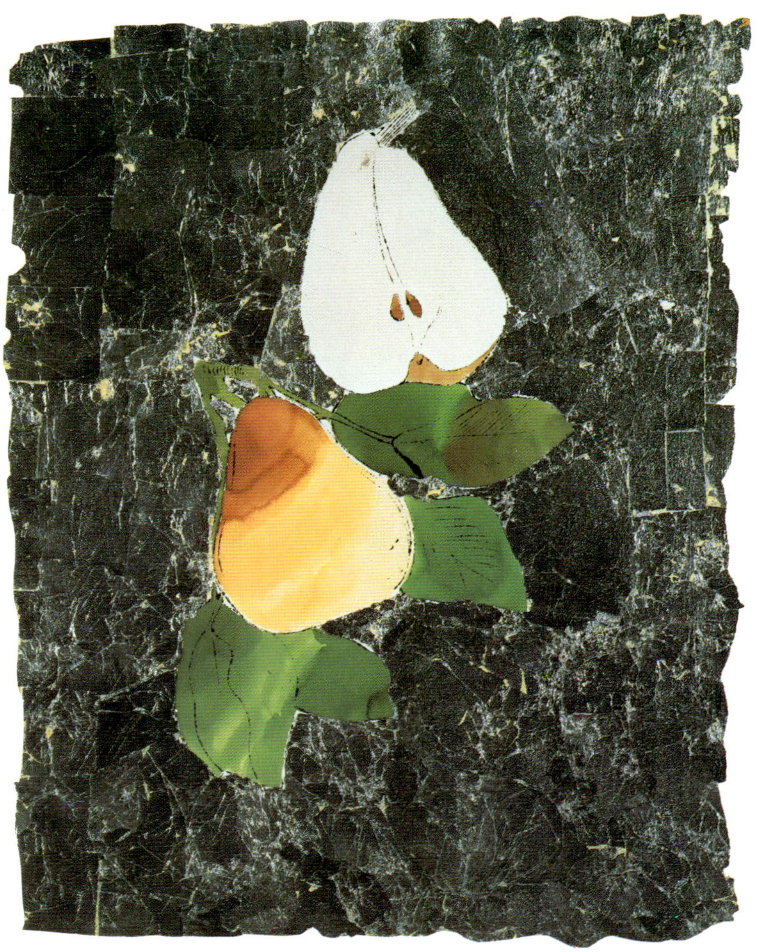

I really like to eat

alone.

I wanted something

more exotic,

like guava.

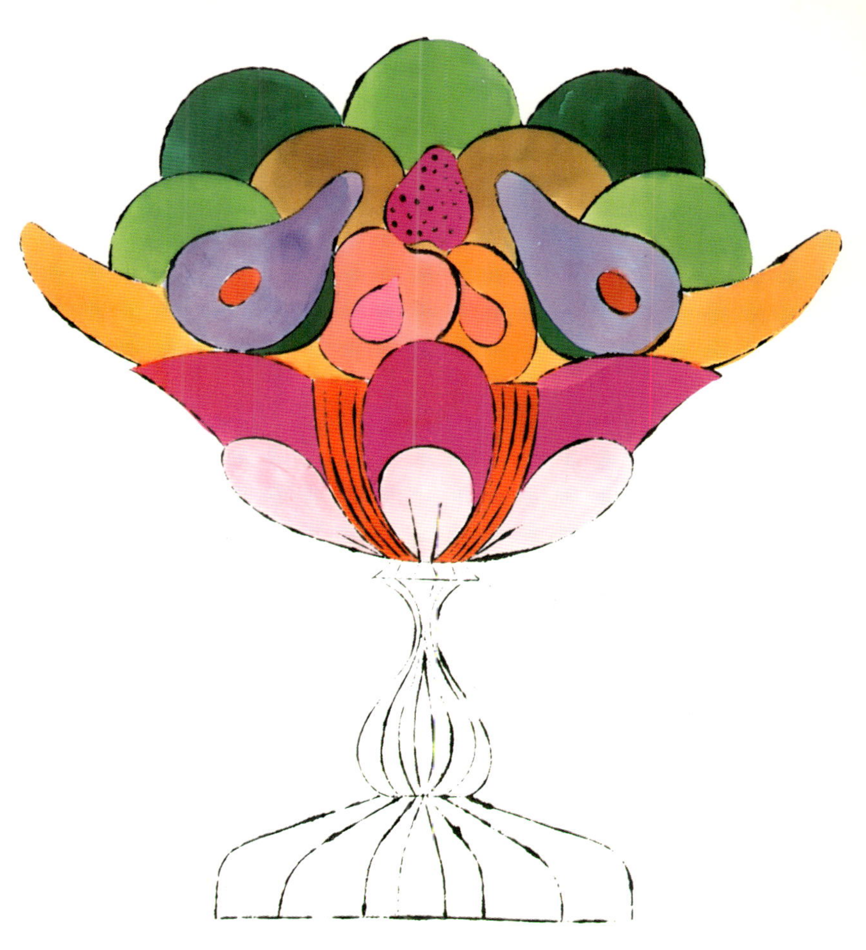

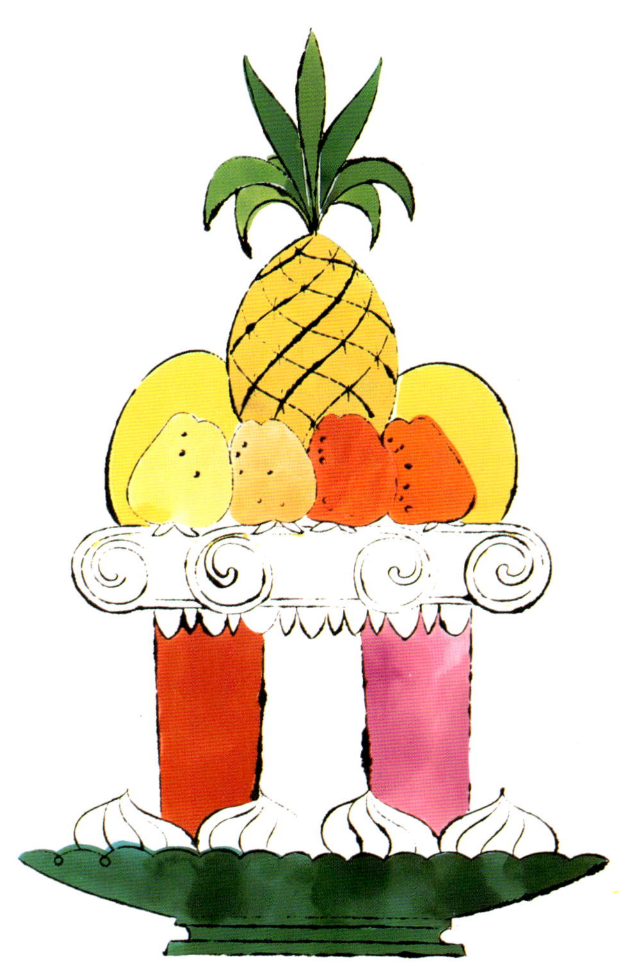

Do you want

pineapple,

papaya,

guava,

peach,

coconut,

apple,

orange,

strawberry,

grapefruit,

pink grapefruit,

cherry-apple,

apple-strawberry,

grape,

piña colada,

sparkling apple or

Juicy Juice?™

Do you want any of this fresh-squeezed?

What's the food?

Did I miss any
good hors d'oeuvres?

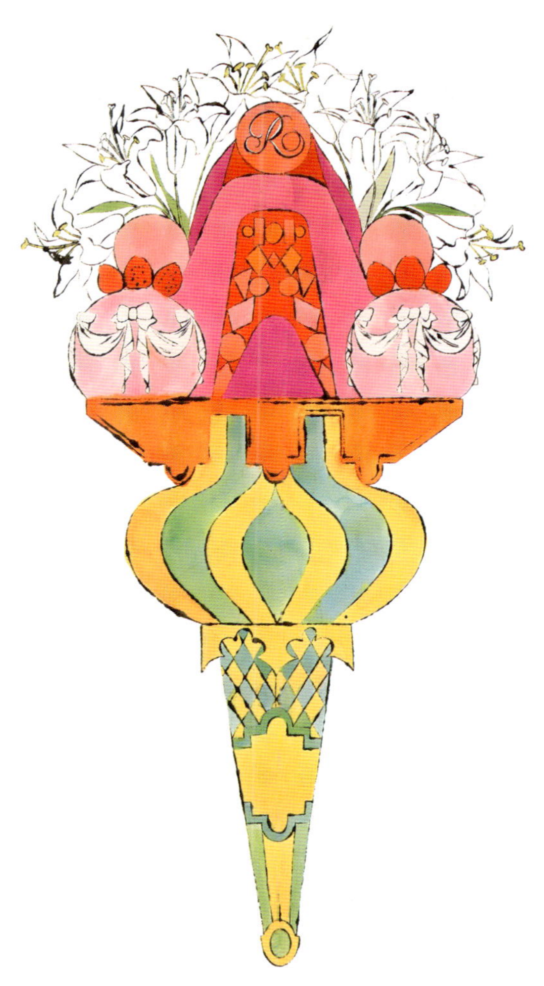

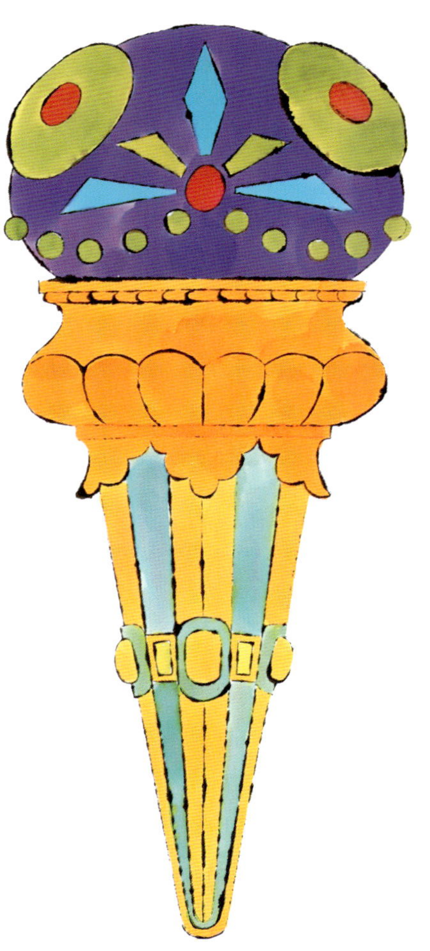

So now
I'm throwing out

all
the
junk
food.

Tab™ is Tab™

and no matter how **rich** you are, you **can't** get a better one.

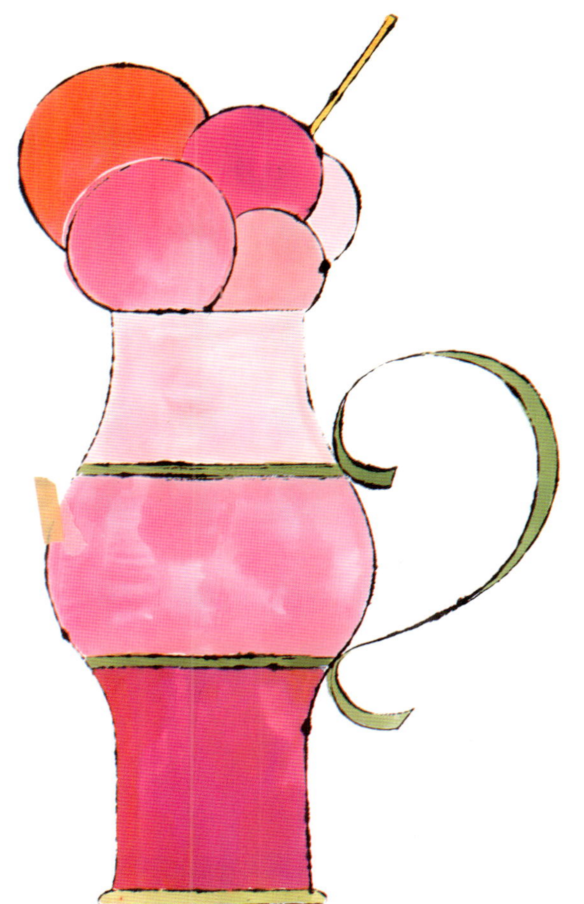

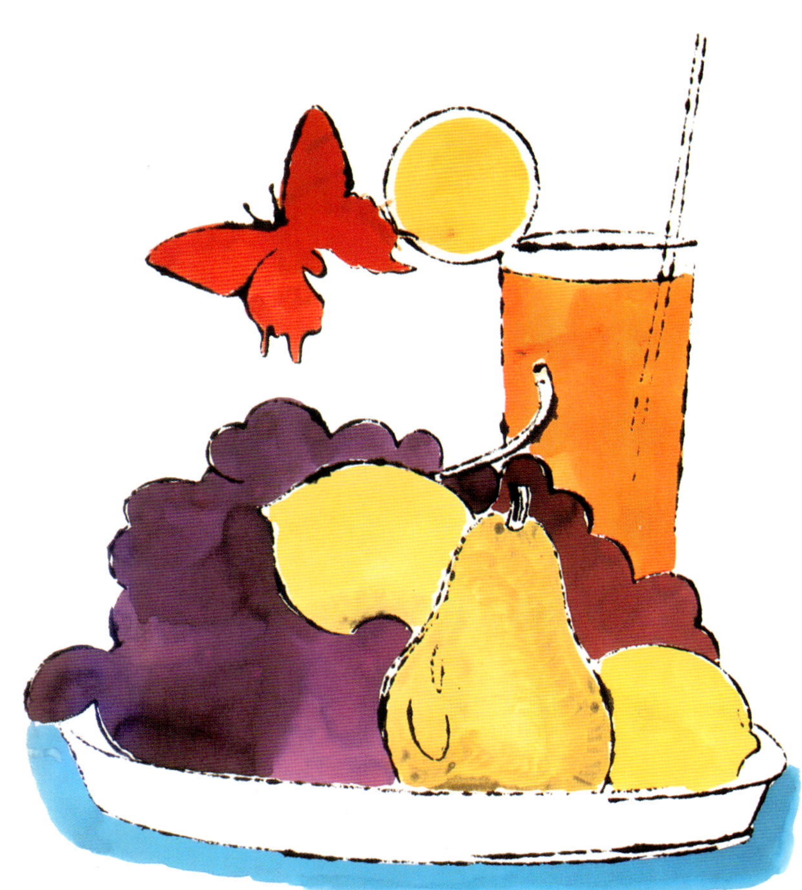

When you want an orange,
you don't want
someone asking you,

"An orange
what?"

He said that only

fish

and chicken

and fresh

vegetables

were good for you.

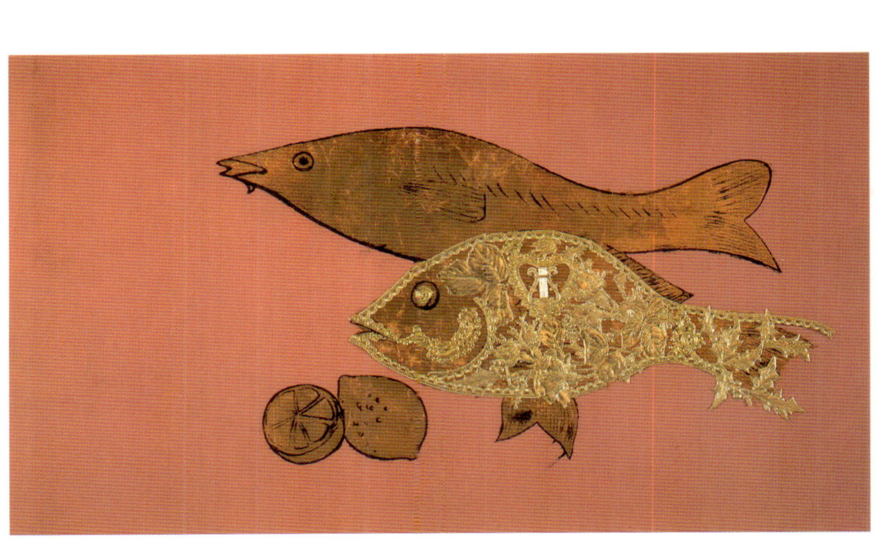

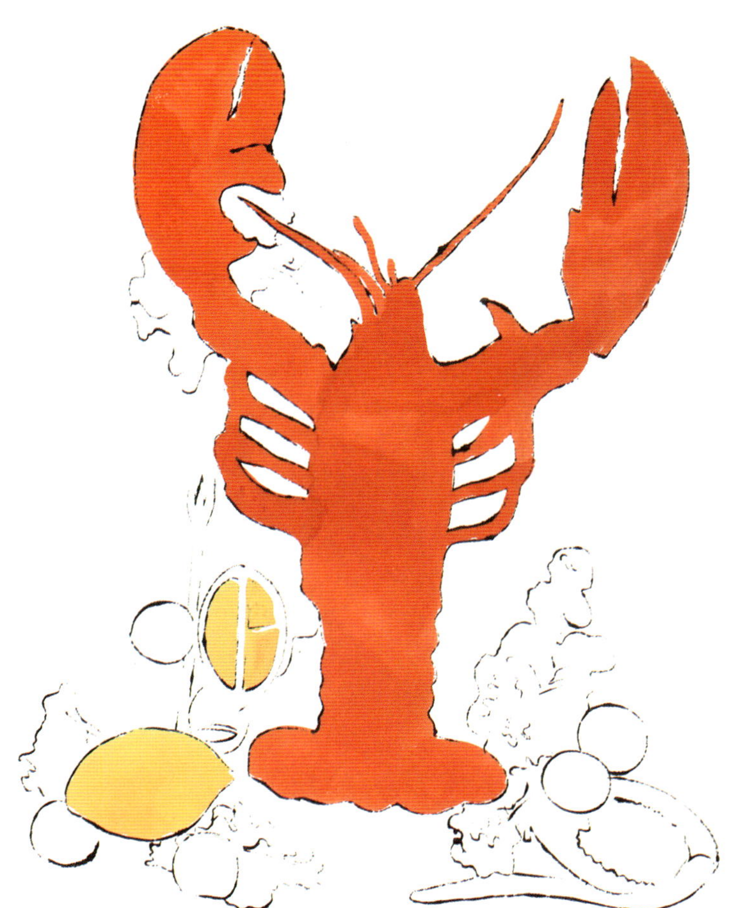

When I see
cold shellfish —
like shrimp
and clams —

that says to me that
somebody really went
all out.

It's nice

to have a little breakfast

made
for
you.

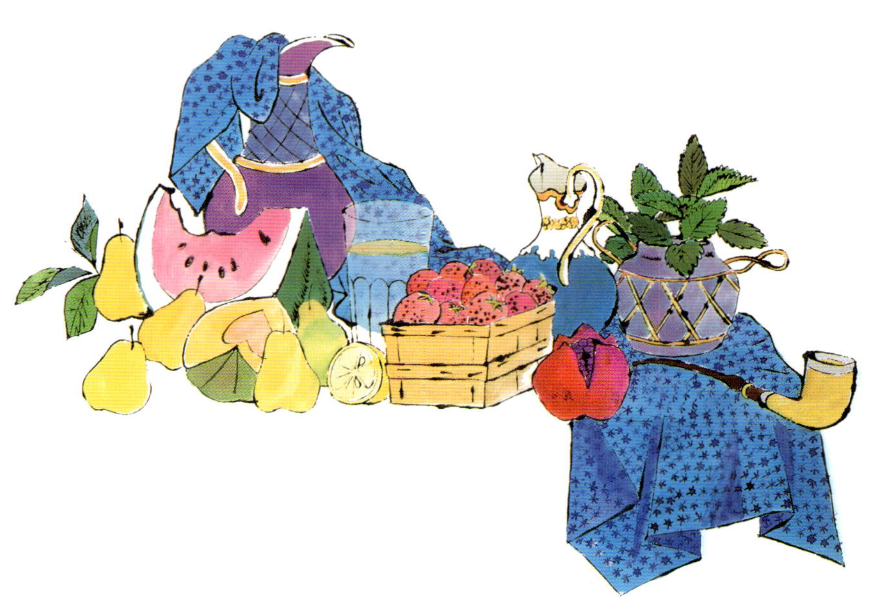

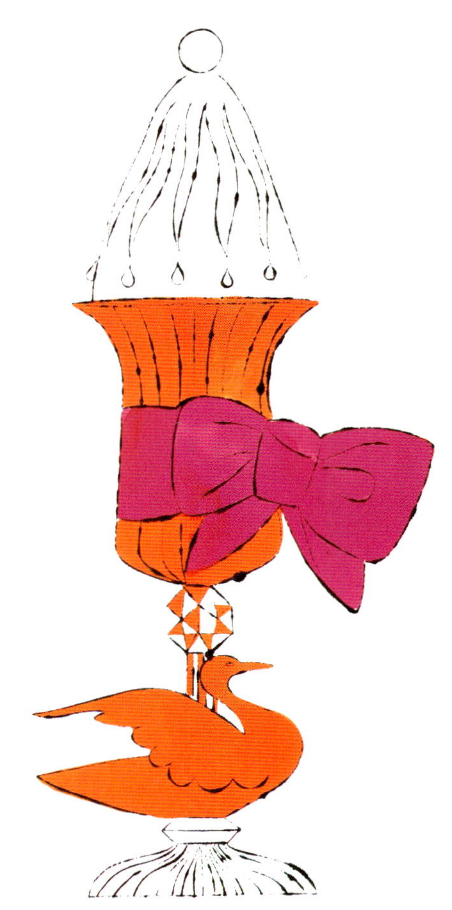

She brought over soup

and bread

and dessert.

I really spoil myself
in the food area,

so my leftovers are often

grand.

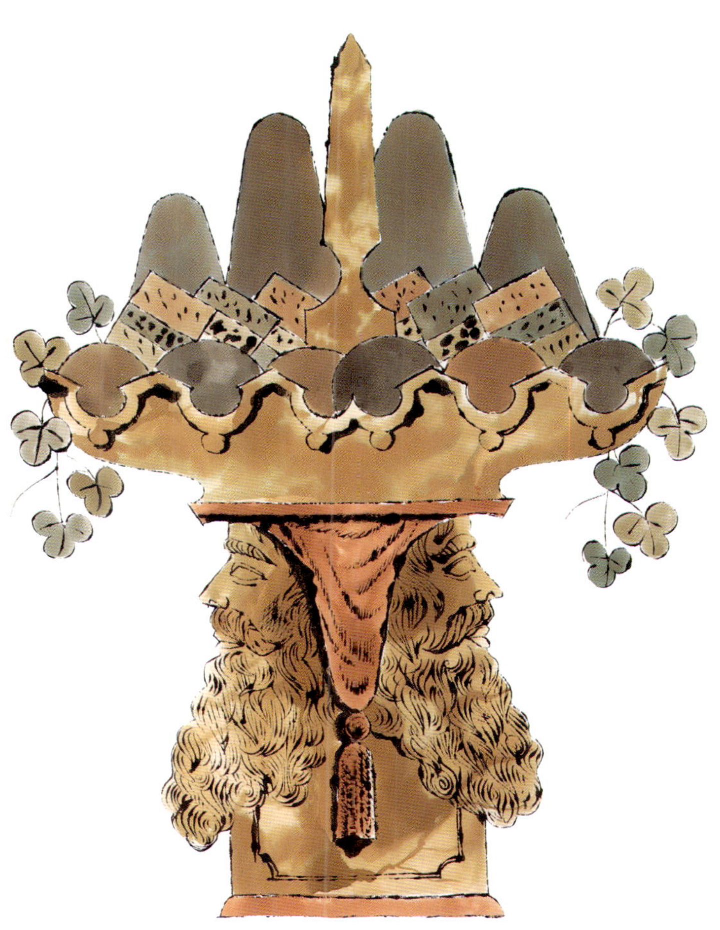

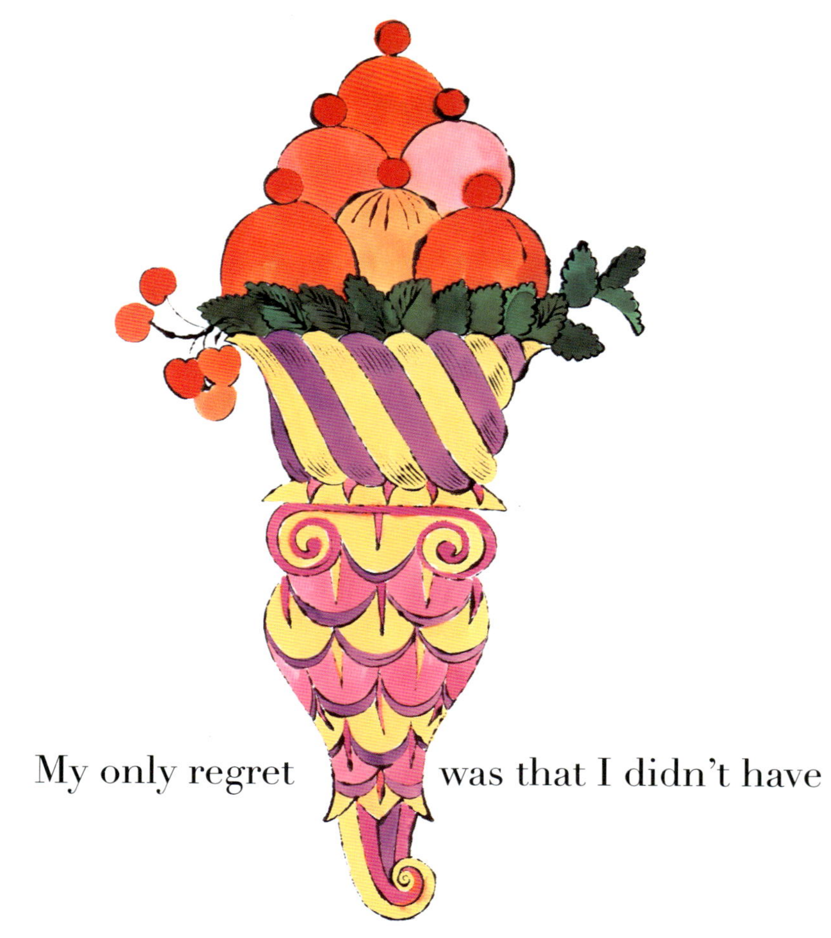

My only regret was that I didn't have

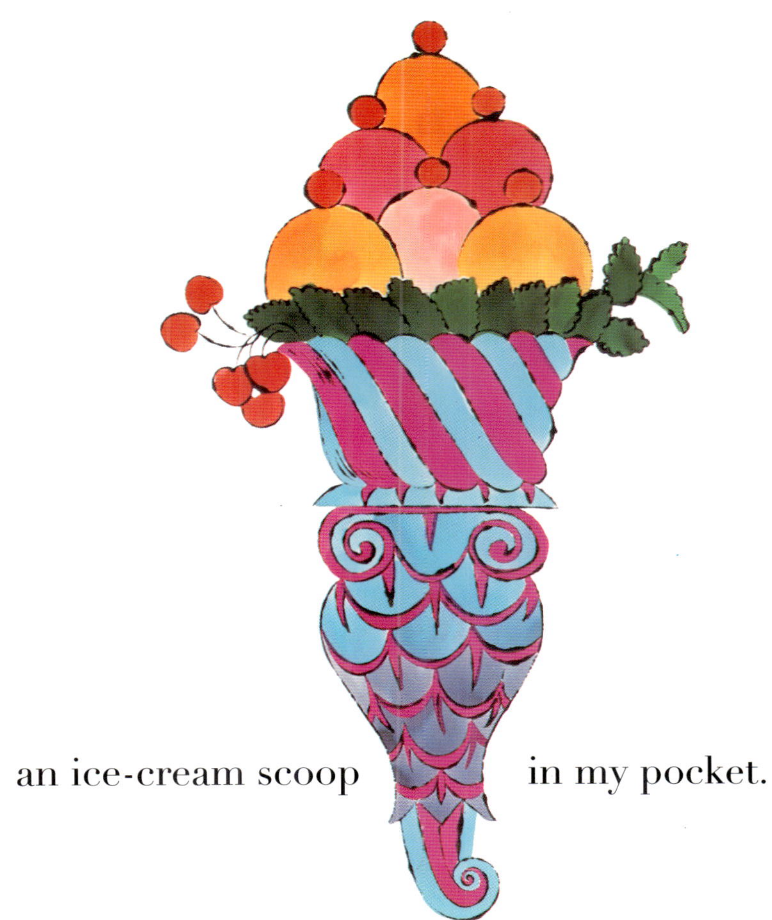

an ice-cream scoop   in my pocket.

What can I give her?

Some chocolate?

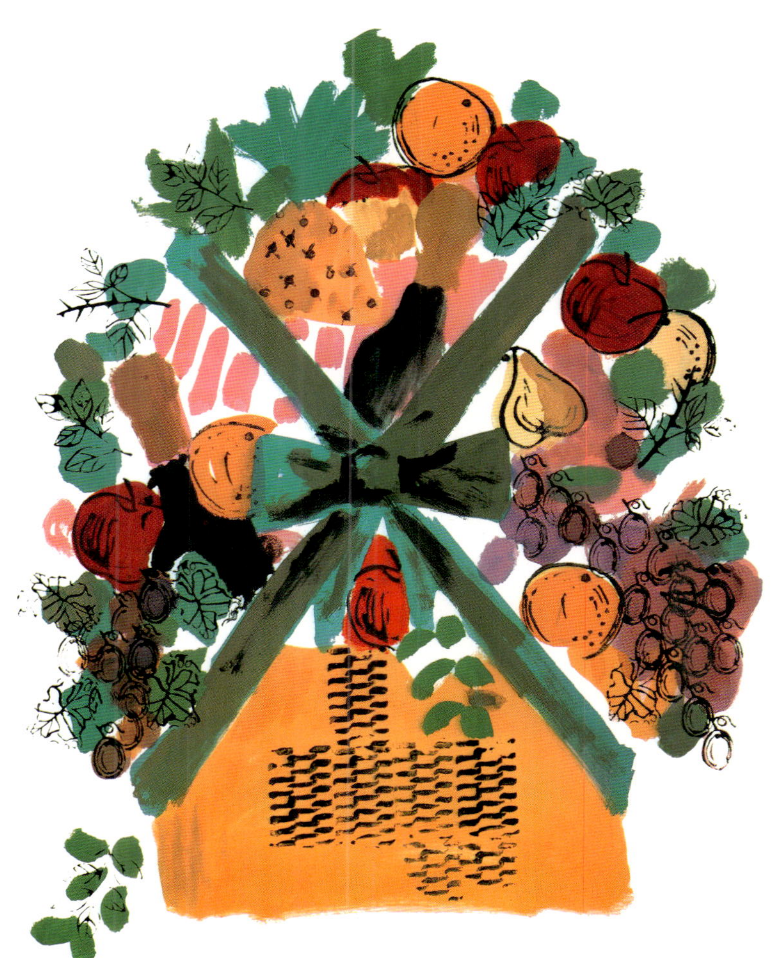

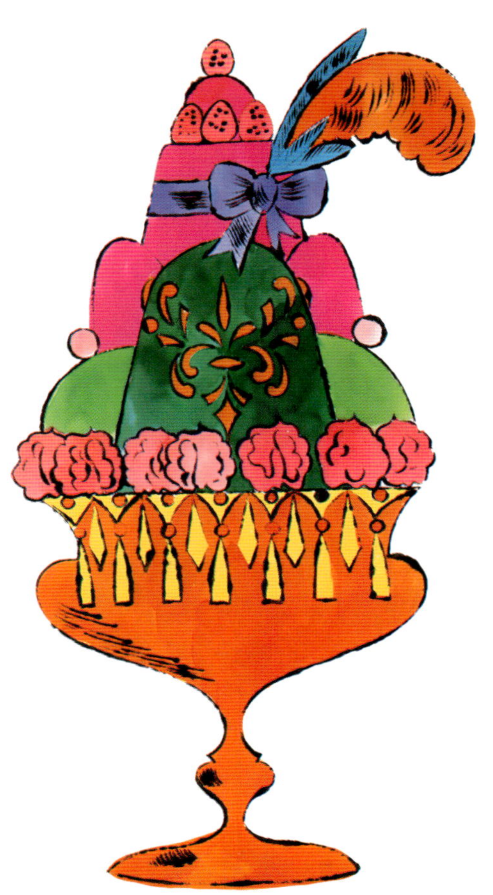

After he saw **the bill,** he stopped making fun of the meal.

Those were the restaurants

I truly loved the most—

ones just like

Schrafft's.

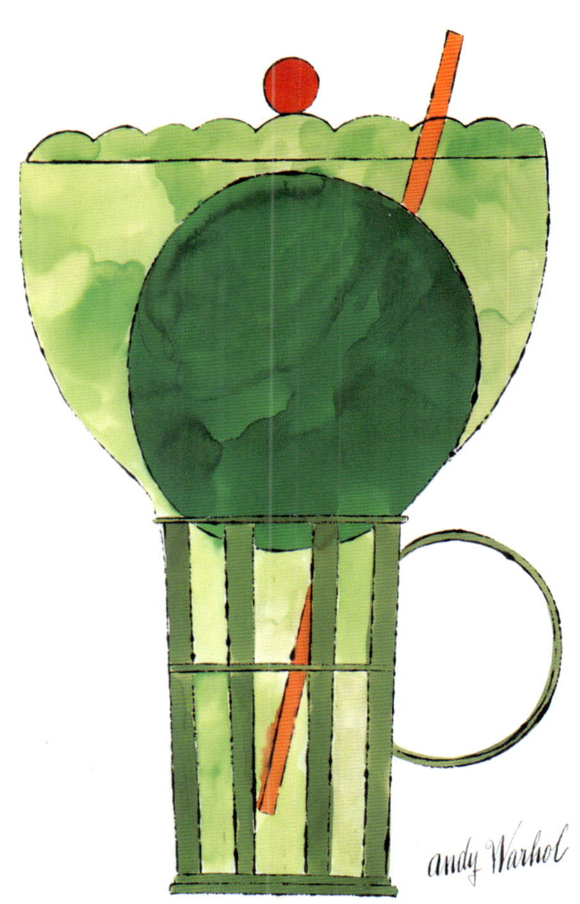

andy Warhol

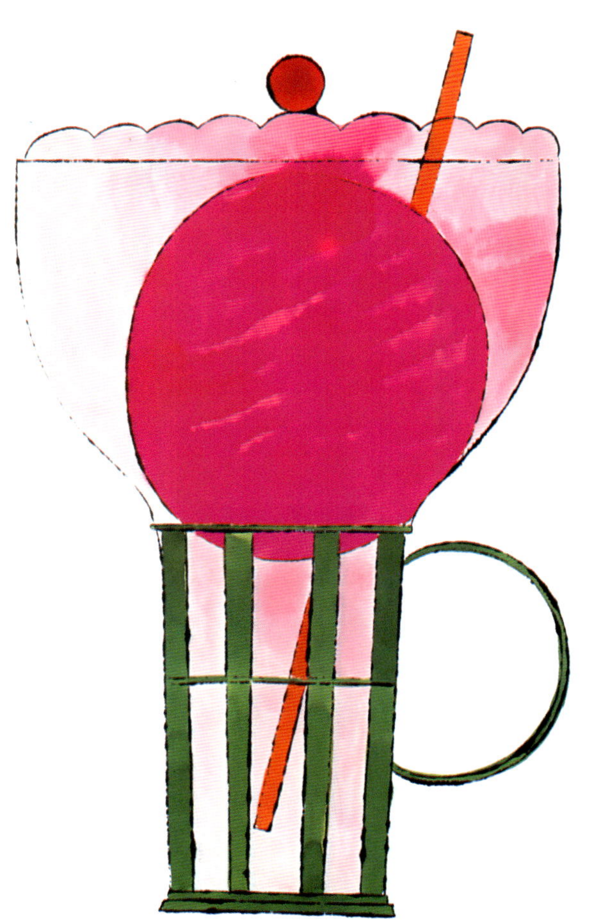

There were eighteen different desserts.

They
didn't even notice

the
cake.

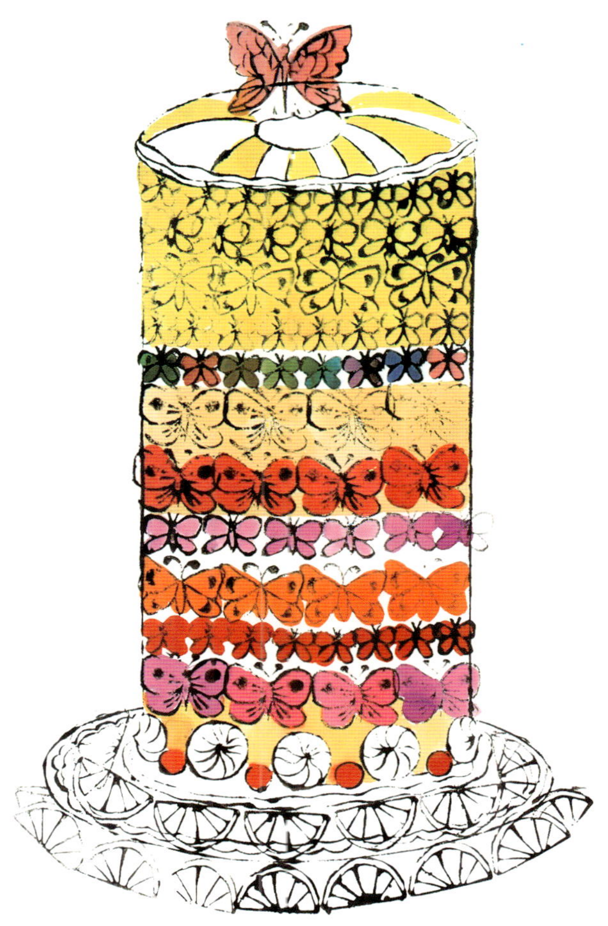

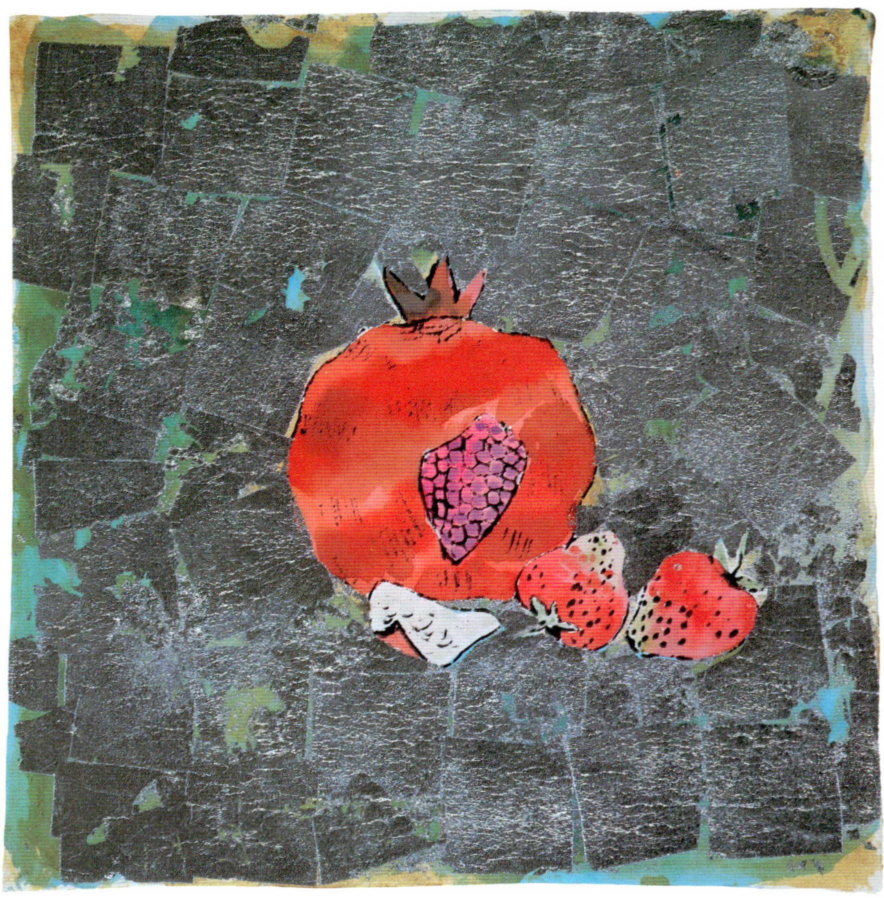

We sat around

eating lots

of fruit that we'd

gotten for lunches

so it wouldn't go bad over the weekend.

I love

the way the smell of each fruit

gets into the rough wood of the crates

and into the tissue-paper wrappings.

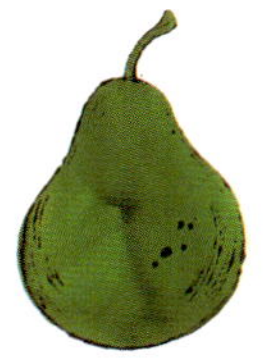
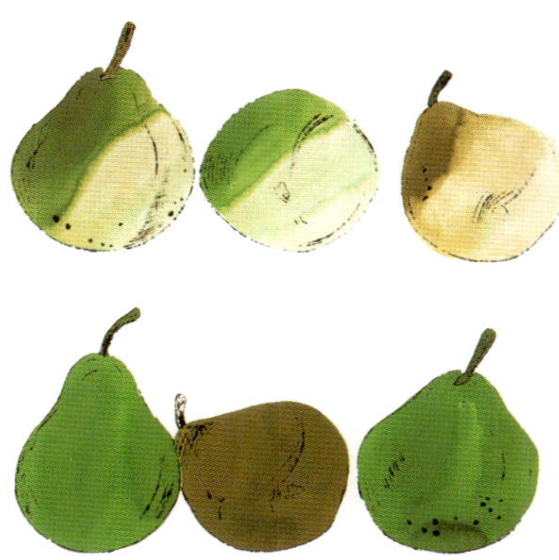

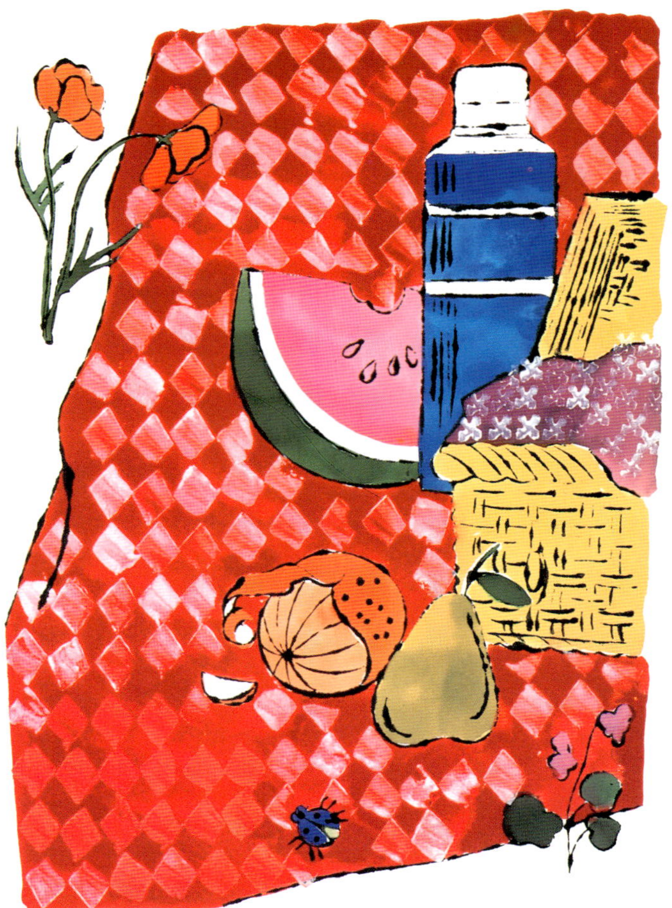

You just
throw open the doors
to the garden
and eat out
in the open air
with flowers and trees
all around.

That's the hard part of overdosing on cherries —

you

have

all

the

pits

to tell you exactly
how many you ate.

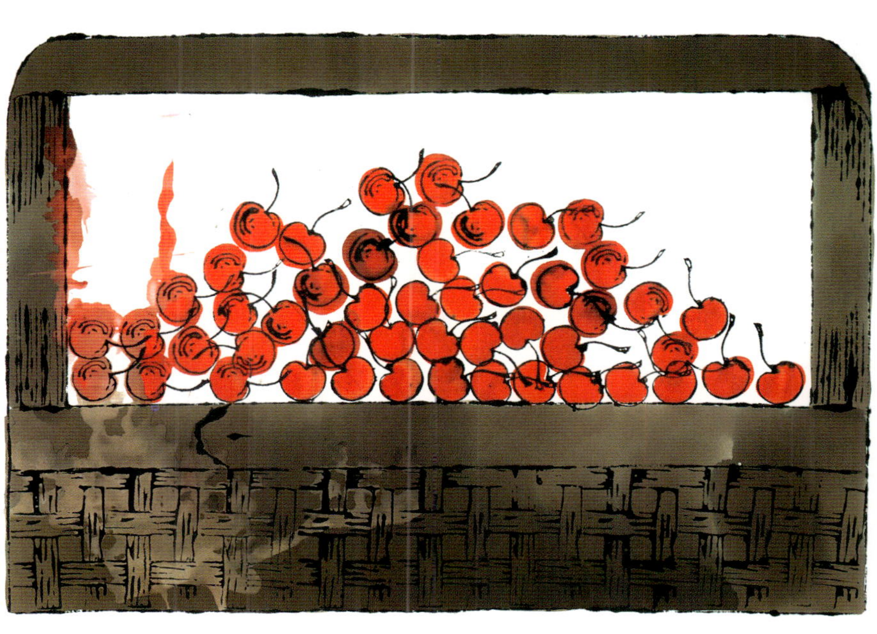

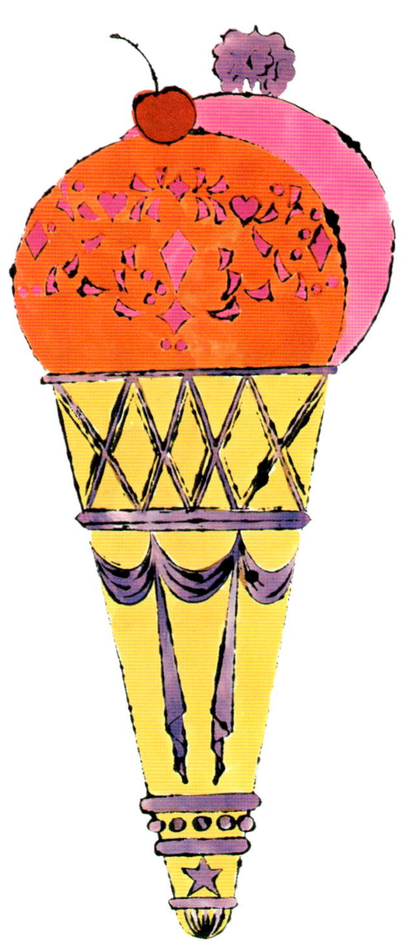

I'm only kidding myself
when I go through
the motions of
cooking protein:

all I ever really want is *sugar.*

Progress

is very important

and exciting

in

everything

except food.

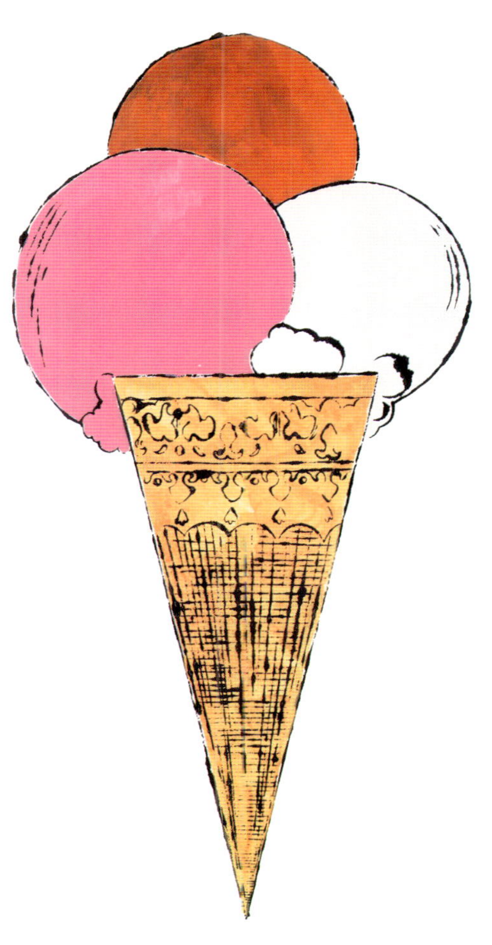

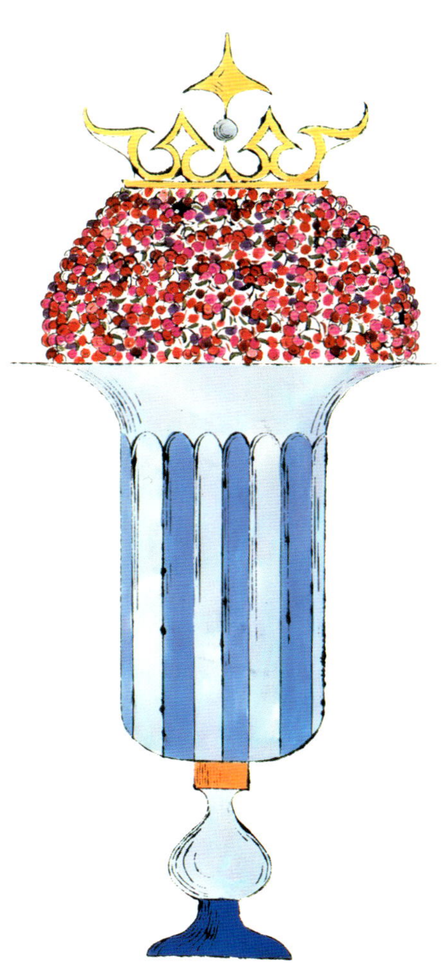

People
are really split
on whether food is everything
at a party
or nothing.

Try the Andy Warhol New York City Diet:

when I order in a restaurant, I order everything that **I don't want,** so I have a lot to play around with while everyone else eats.

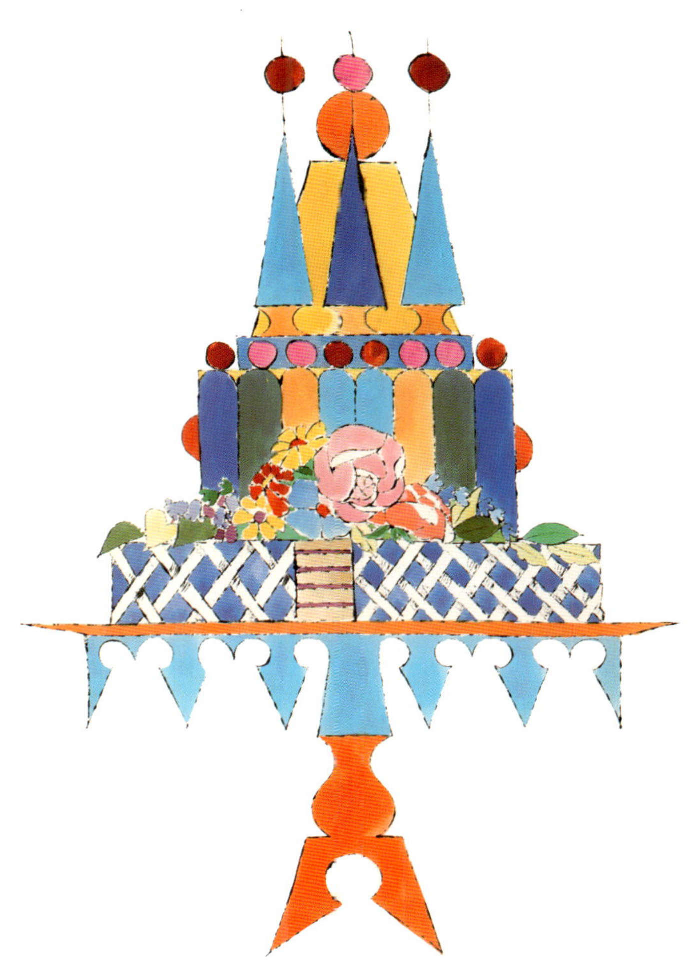

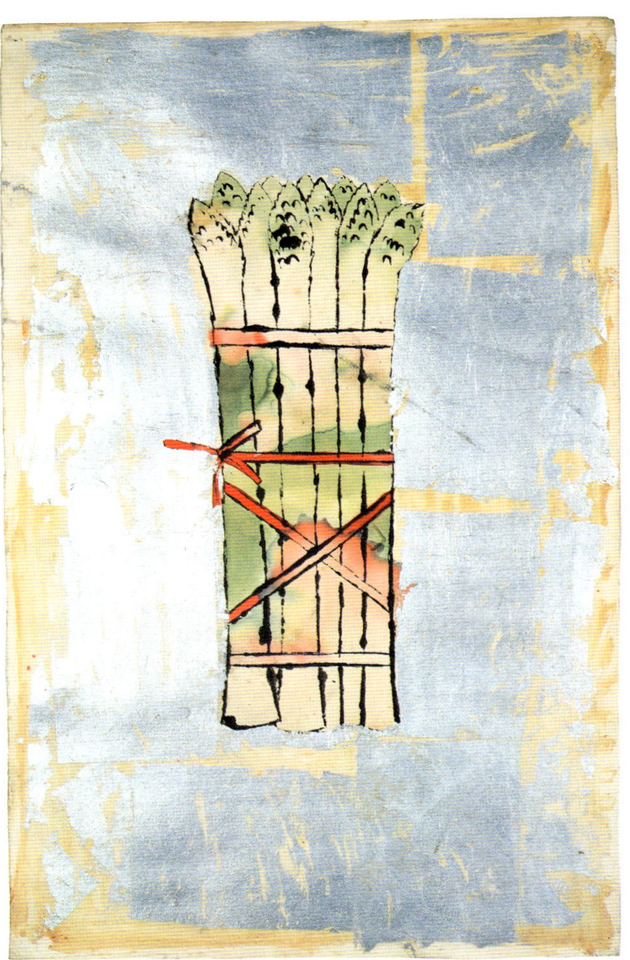

My favorite
simultaneous
action is

talking while eating.

I think
it's a sign
of class.

I just planted myself in front of it

and ate and ate and ate.

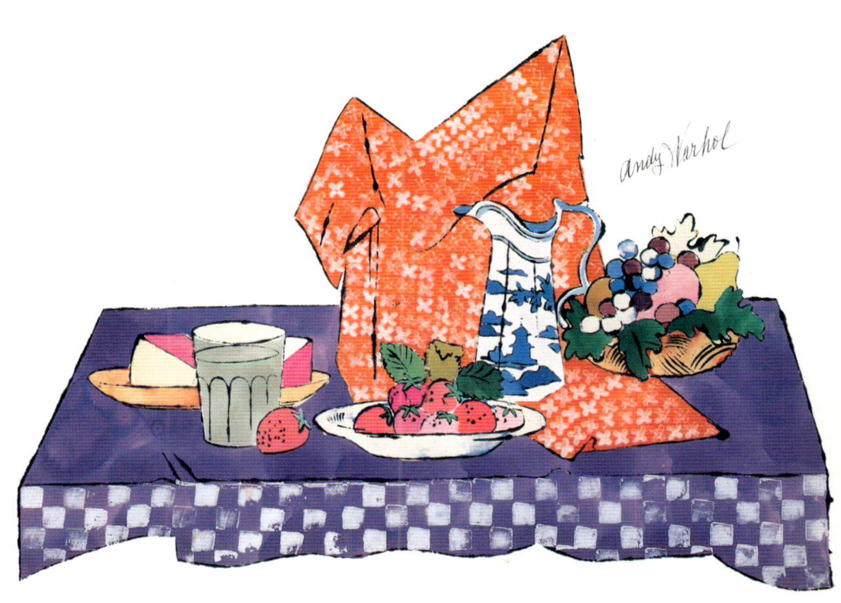

Andy Warhol

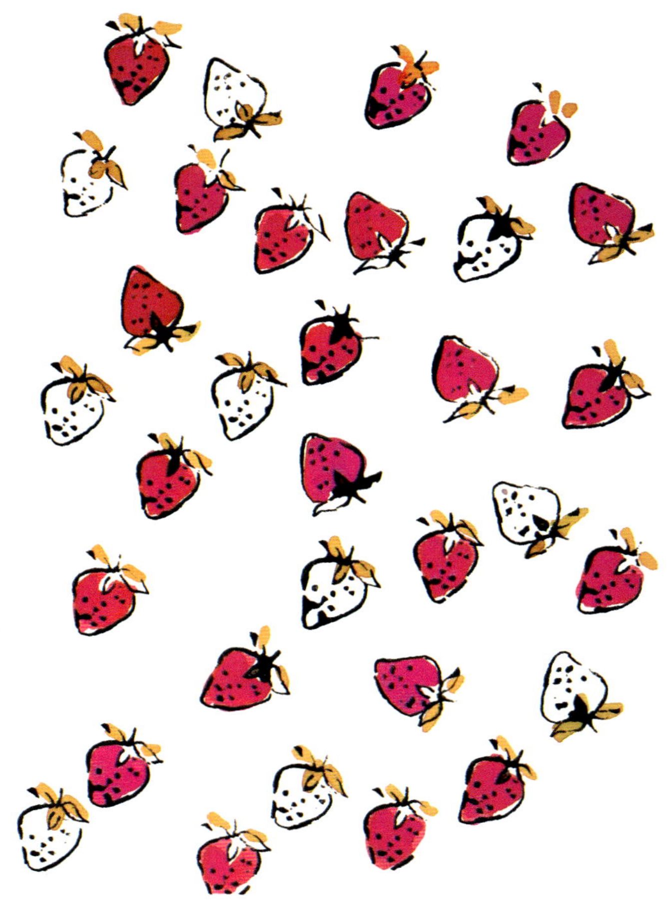

If there's giant

strawberries,

I'll just stand there and eat

one after the

other.

It's always my turn to talk just when I've filled my mouth.

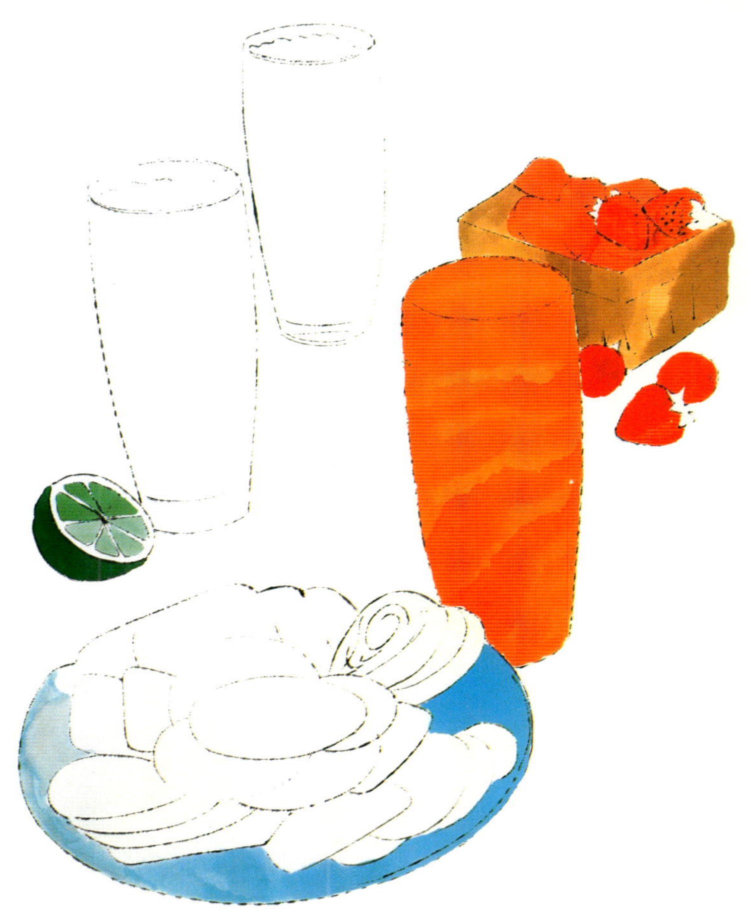

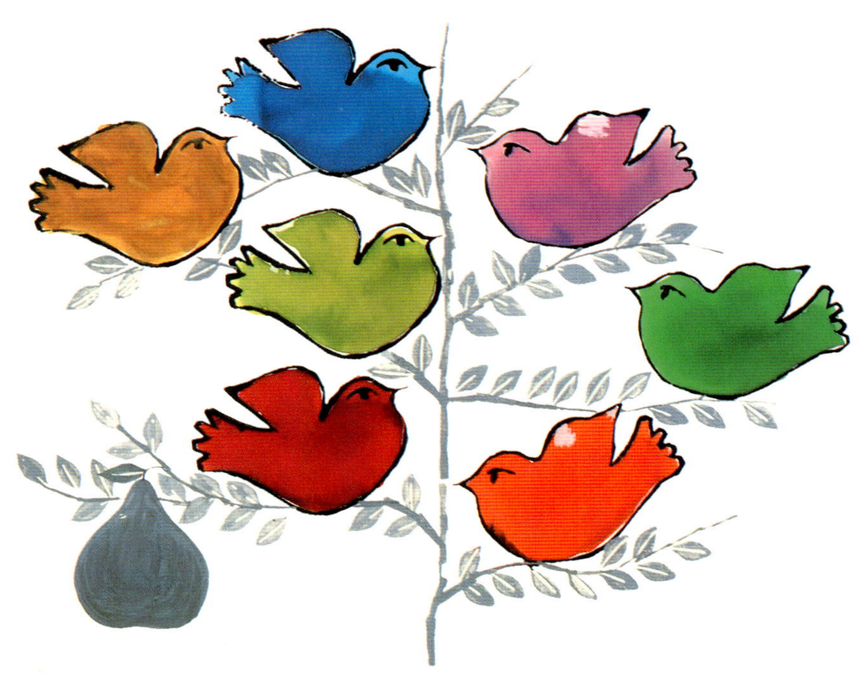

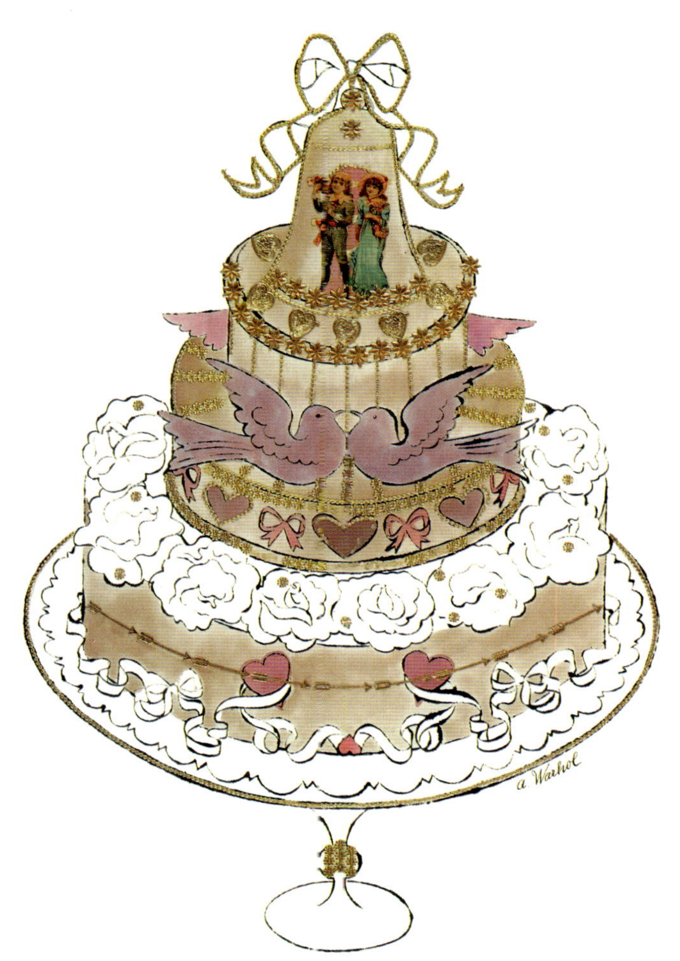
a. Warhol

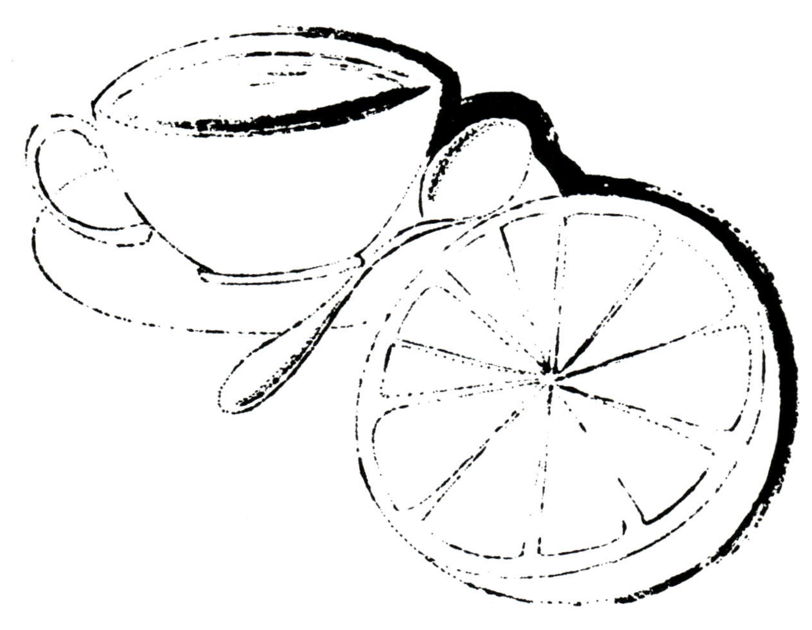

All quotations are by Andy Warhol
and were first published as follows:

Pages 7, 8, 11, 12, 23, 28, 32, 48, 51, 52, 55, 56, 60, 63, 68:
Andy Warhol. *The Philosophy of Andy Warhol (from A to B
and Back Again).* New York: Harcourt Brace Jovanovich, 1975.

Pages 15, 20:
Andy Warhol. *America.* New York: Harper & Row, 1985.

Pages 16, 27, 59, 64, 67:
Andy Warhol and Pat Hackett. *Andy Warhol's Party Book.*
New York: Crown Publishers, 1988.

Pages 19, 24, 31, 34–35, 36, 39, 43, 44, 47:
Pat Hackett, Editor. *The Andy Warhol Diaries.* New York:
Warner Books, 1989.

Page 40:
Andy Warhol. *POPism: The Warhol '60s.* New York: Harcourt
Brace Jovanovich, 1980.

Captions by page number

Cover
   Untitled (Ice Cream Dessert),
   c. 1959
   Ink and ink wash on
   Strathmore paper
   29" x 23"

Endpapers
   Untitled (Stamped Pears), c. 1960
   Ink and graphite on ivory laid
   paper
   17 7/8" x 11 3/4"

3   *Ice Cream Dessert,* c. 1959
    Ink and ink wash on
    Strathmore paper
    29" x 23"

5   *Untitled (Stamped Cherries),*
    c. 1960
    Ink, graphite, and ink wash on
    ivory paper
    17 7/8" x 12"

6   *Untitled (Still Life),* c. 1957
    Ink, ink wash, and tempera on
    Strathmore paper
    28 5/8" x 22 1/2"

9   *Ice Cream Dessert,* c. 1959
    Ink, ink wash, and tempera on
    Strathmore paper
    29" x 23"

10 *Untitled (Two Pears),* c. 1957
    Silver leaf, ink, and ink wash
    on Strathmore paper
    14 1/2" x 11 1/4"

13 *Untitled (Ice Cream Dessert),*
    c. 1959
    Ink and ink wash on
    Strathmore paper
    28 5/8" x 22 5/8"

14 *Ice Cream Dessert,* c. 1959
    Ink and ink wash on
    Strathmore paper
    28 5/8" x 22 5/8"

17 *Ice Cream Dessert,* c. 1959
Ink and ink wash on
Strathmore paper
28 5/8" x 22 5/8"

18 *Ice Cream Dessert,* c. 1959
Ink, ink wash, and tempera on
Strathmore paper
40" x 30"

21 *Ice Cream Dessert,* c. 1959
Ink and ink wash on
Strathmore paper
28 5/8" x 22 5/8"

22 *Untitled (Still Life),* c. 1956
Ink and ink wash on
Strathmore paper
14 1/2" x 11 3/8"

25 *Untitled (Two Fish with Lemons),*
c. 1956
Gold leaf, gold trim, and ink
on colored graphic art paper
10 1/2" x 18"

26 *Untitled (Lobster),* c. 1956
Ink and ink wash on
Strathmore paper
21" x 11 3/4"

29 *Untitled (Still Life),* c. 1960
Ink and ink wash on
Strathmore paper
22 5/8" x 28 5/8"

30 *Ice Cream Dessert,* c. 1959
Ink and ink wash on
Strathmore paper
29" x 23"

33 *Ice Cream Dessert,* c. 1959
Ink and ink wash on
Strathmore paper
28 7/8" x 22 7/8"

34 *Ice Cream Dessert,* c. 1959
Ink and ink wash on
Strathmore paper
28 5/8" x 22 5/8"

35   *Ice Cream Dessert*, c. 1959
Ink and ink wash on
Strathmore paper
29" x 23"

37   *Untitled (Stamped Basket of Fruit)*, c. 1960
Ink, ink wash, and tempera on
Strathmore paper
29" x 22 7/8"

38   *Untitled (Ice Cream Dessert)*,
c. 1959
Ink and ink wash on
Strathmore paper
28 5/8" x 22 5/8"

41   *Ice Cream Dessert*, c. 1959
Ink and ink wash on
Strathmore paper
29" x 23"

42   *Untitled (Ice Cream Dessert)*,
c. 1959
Ink and ink wash on
Strathmore paper
28 5/8" x 22 5/8"

45   *Untitled (Butterfly Layered Cake)*,
c. 1959
Ink and ink wash on
Strathmore paper
29" x 23"

46   *Untitled (Pomegranate and Strawberries)*, c. 1957
Silver leaf, ink, and ink wash
on Strathmore paper
11 1/2" x 11"

49   *Untitled (Pears)*, c. 1956
Ink and ink wash on
Strathmore paper
14 1/2" x 23"

50   *Untitled (Still Life)*, c. 1956
Ink, graphite, and ink wash on
Strathmore paper
21 3/4" x 15 7/8"

53   *Untitled (Still Life)*, c. 1960
Ink and ink wash on
Strathmore paper
16 3/8" x 22 1/2"

54 *Ice Cream Dessert*, c. 1959
Ink and ink wash on
Strathmore paper
28 1/2" x 22 3/8"

57 *Untitled (Ice Cream Dessert)*,
c. 1959
Ink and ink wash on
Strathmore paper
28 5/8" x 22 5/8"

58 *Ice Cream Dessert*, c. 1959
Ink and ink wash on
Strathmore paper
29" x 23"

61 *Ice Cream Dessert*, c. 1959
Ink and ink wash on
Strathmore paper
28 7/8" x 22 7/8"

62 *Untitled (Asparagus)*, c. 1957
Silver leaf, ink, and ink wash
on Strathmore paper

65 *Untitled (Still Life)*, c. 1956
Ink and ink wash on
Strathmore paper
17 1/4" x 22 1/2"

66 *Untitled (Stamped Strawberries)*,
c. 1959
Ink and ink wash on
Strathmore paper
9 5/8" x 6 3/4"

69 *Untitled (Still Life)*, c. 1956
Ink and ink wash on
Strathmore paper
20 3/8" x 13 1/4"

70 *Untitled (Birds)*, c. 1959
Ink, graphite, tempera, and ink
wash on Strathmore paper
14 1/2" x 23"

71 *Untitled (Wedding Cake)*, c. 1959
Stamped gold collage, ink, and
ink wash on Strathmore paper
28 5/8" x 22 1/2"

72 *Untitled (Still Life)*, c. 1956
Ink and ink wash on
Strathmore paper
9 3/8" x 11"

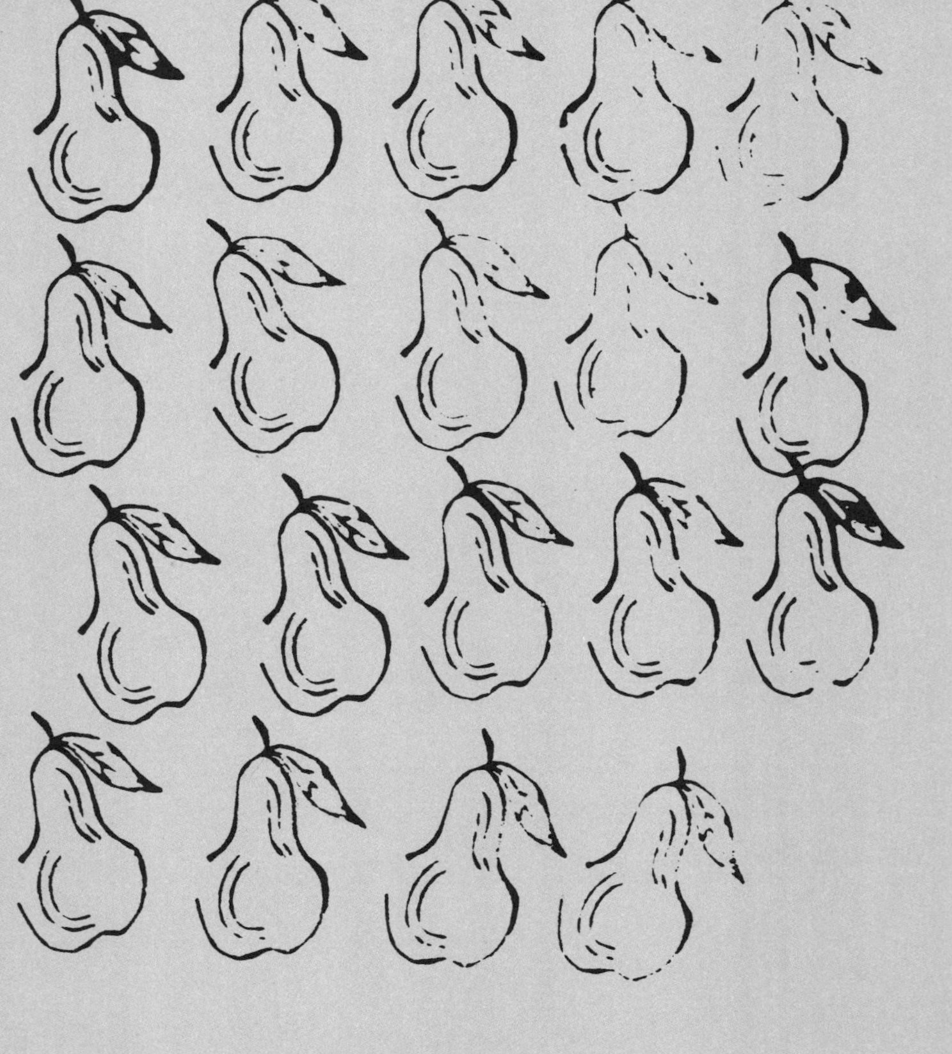